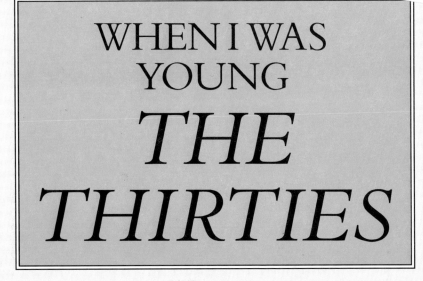

WHEN I WAS YOUNG
THE THIRTIES

NEIL THOMSON
MEETS
GLYN DAVIES

FRANKLIN WATTS
LONDON   NEW YORK   SYDNEY   TORONTO

Glyn Davies was born in 1924 in the Rhondda Valley in South Wales. He lived with his family in the town of Tonypandy and went to school nearby. After leaving school at the age of fourteen, he worked for a year in a local bakery before becoming a miner in the local colliery. He continued to work as a miner during the Second World War and enrolled as a volunteer fire-fighter to help in case of bombing attacks.

Glyn married a girl from the next village and he and his wife, Sally, still live in the area.

In 1980 Glyn was made redundant from his job with the National Coal Board. He is now very active in his village community group.

© Franklin Watts 1991

First published in Great Britain by
Franklin Watts
96 Leonard Street
London
EC2A 4RH

Paperback edition 1993
Franklin Watts Australia
14 Mars Road
Lane Cove
N.S.W. 2066

ISBN: 0 7496 0498 0(hardback)
ISBN: 0 7496 1386 6 (paperback)

CONTENTS

Me and my family

I was born in 1924 in the upstairs bedroom of my parents' house in Tonypandy, South Wales. I was christened Glyndwr Davies but I've always been called Glyn. I had two older sisters, Gwladys and Gwyneth, and an older brother, Thomas. Later on my brother Dilwyn was born. He was seven years younger than me.

My father worked in the Gorki colliery. In those days they used horses to pull the coal trucks along underground. Father was a master haulier, which meant that he was in charge of the men working with the horses underground. His job was to keep the miners supplied with empty trucks ready to be filled with coal.

We lived in a rented house in Charles Street. Ours was the end house at the bottom of the hill. Father always said it was holding up the rest of the street.

Me and Dilwyn in our Sunday best.

My father with my brother Dilwyn in my pedal car. I was lucky to be given it. Mine was the first in the village.

In the early 1930s the collieries were privately owned. Branch lines linked them to the main railway network.

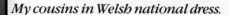

My cousins in Welsh national dress.

Our house was like nearly all the other miners' houses in the Rhondda Valley. We had a front room and a kitchen downstairs and three bedrooms upstairs. There was no bathroom, only a cold water tap in the house and an outdoor toilet. We had gas lighting downstairs and in the front bedroom. If you slept in the other rooms you had to take a candle upstairs with you.

Mother cooked on the open fire in the kitchen. We had a coal-burning grate with the oven next to it. It was polished with black lead to make it gleam.

There was no carpet in the house. We had either coconut matting or rag-rugs made from strips of old clothes sewn onto a potato sack. Mother would buy a pennyworth of sand and scour the flagstones in the kitchen. She also cleaned the front doorstep and a stretch of the pavement outside.

The children from our street at the end of the 1920s. My two sisters are to the left of the middle row. The photo was taken from outside our house.

My childhood home now. I live in a house just up the street.

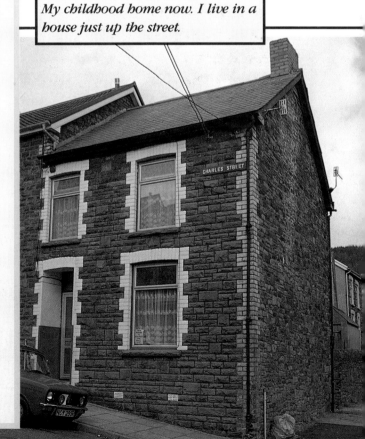

5

My sister Gwyneth was a great polisher. She kept the wooden floor in the front room, which we called the parlour, really shiny. Once when the doctor came to visit my mother, he slipped and fell over on the shiny floor! Mother was resting by the fire in the parlour at the time. The fire was only lit in there at Christmas, or if someone was unwell.

Me and my brothers helped around the house with a few jobs. Father would order a ton of coal to be tipped outside and I'd have to help cart it up the four steps into the coal shed. The one thing we weren't short of was coal.

We had a small garden which Father and I looked after. One year we planted potatoes, cabbages and swedes and the next day went off for an outing. It was dark by the time we got home. Next morning we saw some sheep had escaped into the garden and eaten the lot! We only got a few potatoes out of it. After that we just kept it tidy. The sheep put a damper on us doing any more gardening.

Coal burning stoves were used for cooking and heating water in the 1930s.

The sheep were in the street all the time when I was young. There were more sheep than dogs.

Park View Terrace Abercwmboi

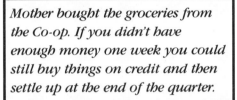

Mother bought the groceries from the Co-op. If you didn't have enough money one week you could still buy things on credit and then settle up at the end of the quarter.

In the 1930s women mostly worked in the home or in domestic service.

Mother did all the cooking and the meals were the same each week. Monday we ate cooked meat from Sunday; Tuesday was fish and home-made chips; Wednesday was lamb chops; Thursday was cold meat and salad. (I was always made to eat the salad. I've been off it ever since.) Friday was home-made faggots and mushy peas bought from a woman down the road; Saturday was bacon and egg. Finally, on Sundays we ate beef, potatoes, peas and cabbage, followed by spotted dick or jam roly-poly.

Some Sundays, for a treat, we had rice pudding or Mother opened a tin of fruit and we had that with condensed milk. In wintertime we had broth or pea soup on a Thursday instead of cold meat.

Hardly anything came in a packet. Most people made their own cakes and jams. A tin of biscuits was kept in the kitchen but we couldn't just help ourselves. We used to sneak in but if Mother caught us we'd get a clip around the ear.

Down the pit

Like nine out of ten men in our valley, my father worked in a colliery. It was difficult to find other work. Once you were fourteen, you left school on a Friday and went down the pit on the Monday. Or if you were clever enough you could train to become a teacher or a preacher.

The pit where my father worked was very near our house. He came home at the end of a shift covered from head to foot with black dust. Mother always had the hot water ready for his bath and then cooked his tea. If his clothes were wet from the pit they had to be hung in front of the fire.

There was never much room at home. But we were better off than a lot of families who had lodgers to help pay the rent. The men often had to share beds. There'd be the day shift and the night shift at the pit and they'd swap over beds between shifts. You were considered a bit posh if your family had the whole house to themselves.

The work underground was always dirty and dangerous. Safety helmets and dust masks were rare in the 1930s.

You should see me on Sunday!

JOHN KNIGHT'S
FAMILY HEALTH SOAP

There were few collieries with pit-head baths in the 1930s. Miners had to wait until they got home to wash.

School

When I was four I went to the local school in Llwynypia, a few minutes walk down the hill. It was a mixed school but boys and girls had separate classrooms. From four-to-seven years old we had women teachers. After that the boys had men teachers and the women taught the girls. We had lots of respect for the teachers. We always called them "Sir" or "Miss" if we saw them out on the street in the evenings.

The teachers were pretty strict and I was caned quite a lot. If I was caught talking in class the teacher would say "hand out" and I'd get the cane just on the tip of my fingers. Then when I got home Mother would give me a clip on the ear as well for being naughty at school.

There were between thirty and forty boys in my class but often a lot were away because of illness. Influenza, chickenpox, smallpox and measles were quite common then.

Llwynypia School now. The buildings have changed very little since the 1930s.

The log book from Glyn's school.

The twin sisters (shown at centre) of my wife-to-be, Sally, received prizes for good attendance.

Most days the timetable was the same. In the morning we started at nine o'clock with arithmetic and moved on to history and geography. We went home for dinner at twelve and then came back at half-past one. In the afternoons we did dictation, reading and composition. We had two break-times a day in the yard – a quarter-of-an-hour in the morning, and the same in the afternoon.

We had half-an-hour a week in Welsh. I was hopeless at that and always got nought out of ten. My father understood Welsh but didn't speak it much. My mother didn't understand it at all.

In the 1930s many primary schools were overcrowded. Up to forty children might be in one class.

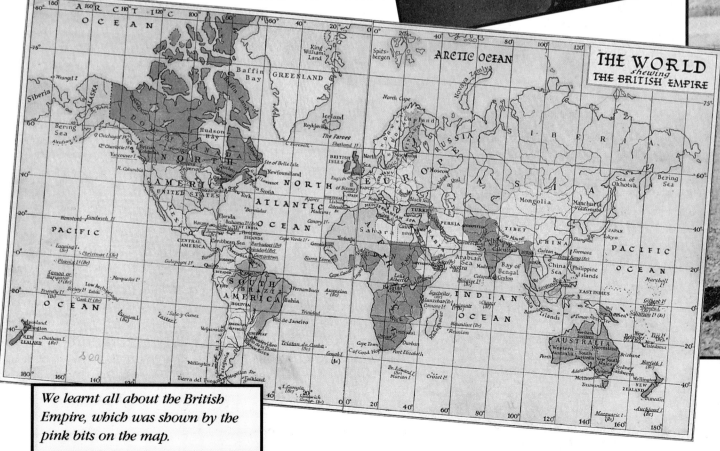

We learnt all about the British Empire, which was shown by the pink bits on the map.

Llwynypia School Scholarships 1940.

R. Samuel. K. Arthur. V. Morgan G. Brooks. D. Nash. G. Bone. J. Dallimore. M. Thomas. H. Griffiths.
D. Morgan. J. Thomas Mr. R. Bowen. N. Evans M. Jones.

Children leaving Llwynypia School with scholarships.

We wore special clothes for school. When we came home we changed into any old patched things just to save the school clothes. All our clothes were handed on from one child to the next.

I was never brilliant at school. There were exams at the end of each summer term and if you didn't pass you had to stay down a year. Somehow I just managed to scrape through each time.

We had one lesson a week in woodwork, and had to walk to a nearby school for it. I made a stool once which I thought was perfect. I took it home and felt quite proud. My father came back from work, had his bath in front of the fire and then sat down on the stool. All the legs broke off and he collapsed on the floor. He called me everything under the sun. He was so cross!

The brightest children won scholarships to go on to secondary school. Otherwise, few parents could afford to keep more than one child at school after they were fourteen. Once you started work you had to give your parents some of your wages each week.

Sundays

Sunday was a special day, it was the only time the collieries were closed. We put on our best suits, or rather our only suits, and went to chapel.

I went to Sunday school in the Bethania Chapel in Tonypandy. The service was in Welsh and, since I couldn't speak it very well, I didn't concentrate much. I had to go though. All the children were regulars at one chapel or another.

There were dozens of chapels and churches in the Rhondda. You could have fitted all the people who lived in the valley into chapels all at once and still have seats left over.

Mother was a staunch follower of chapel. She kept a bible in the parlour on a little table along with a flower vase. She sang in the choir and went along to sisterhood meetings every Tuesday and Thursday night, as well as to all the services on Sunday.

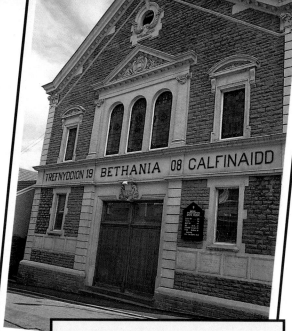

The Bethania chapel in Tonypandy is still in use. Many other chapels in the Rhondda have closed.

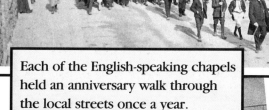

Each of the English-speaking chapels held an anniversary walk through the local streets once a year.

Welsh-speaking chapels held festivals of religious songs every year. The choirs were an important part of social life in the Valley communities.

Every year the Sunday school ran an outing to the seaside at Porthcawl or Barry. The preacher always gave each child a newly-minted threepenny bit to spend during the day.

As soon as we arrived we'd all have a cup of tea and a sandwich. Then we'd go down to the beach and put all the beach chairs in a big circle. We had to play inside the circle so we wouldn't get lost.

We were allowed to paddle in the sea but only up to our ankles. Our mothers were frightened that we might drown if we went swimming in the sea. I never learnt to swim, though some of my friends did.

We never went in the cafe unless it started raining. We just took flasks of tea and sandwiches for everyone. We always ended up in the funfair. Mother gave me money for the rides, 2d or 3d they were. After dinner we sang songs and hymns and then went to catch the bus home.

In the 1930s very few people owned cars. Charabancs or coaches were the only way to get to the seaside.

I always liked going on the helter-skelter at Porthcawl. Funfairs were really popular, even during the war.

Porthcawl in the 1930s.

Games and entertainment

We played lots of different games outside in the lane that ran between the rows of houses. We were safe there from the grown-ups. If we played out the front we had to be careful. Hopscotch in the street was a favourite but if you chalked outside someone's house, the chances were they'd come and chase you away. That included my mother. Everyone was so keen on keeping the streets clean in those days.

Sometimes if a grown-up had been bothering us during a game we'd get our own back. We'd go to his house when he was asleep after the night shift. For devilment reasons we'd stuff paper up the mouth of the drainpipe and light it. The hot air going up made a sound like a ship's hooter and would wake up the fellow upstairs. We didn't hang about for long after that!

There was never much spare money in our street. I did a newspaper round when I was ten. I used the money to buy comics. The Dandy *or* The Beano *were the best.*

I collected cigarette cards; ships and planes were my favourites. We swapped them at school so as to get a complete set. We played a game flicking them against the wall – you could win extra ones that way.

Boys in the Rhondda in the 1930s.

MONOPOLY
THE NEW GAME
AND THE
RAGE OF AMERICA
MILLIONS NOW PLAYING IT

Monopoly was first designed in the 1930s and came from America originally.

CIGARETTES

WILLS'S CIGARETTES

VACUUM-OPERATED TURNTABLE

ROYAL PRINCESSES

We made up lots of games with things that we found lying around. We used to make a skipping rope from the cord that came tied round boxes of oranges. Three of those tied together would stretch from one side of the road to the other.

We played hook and wheel. If we were lucky the colliery blacksmith would make us a wheel. We had a metal hook to go with it to make it spin along the road. We got ball bearings from the colliery and played with them. We dug three or four holes in the lane behind the houses and played something like marbles.

We had to be in by five o'clock in the winter and by half-eight in the summer. If our parents had to shout for us a second time we'd get a clip around the ear.

Children playing with hook and wheel in Clydach Vale earlier in the 20th century. The game was still popular in the 1930s.

When we were playing football in the street we'd keep a look out for the policeman's helmet. Where we lived the policemen were all six-footers. If we saw one we'd all scatter. We'd never stand up to a policeman. If we broke a window we had to pay for it out of our pocket money, so we made sure that didn't happen too often.

On Sunday afternoons Charles Street fielded a football team that went up the mountain to play. We weren't really meant to go and play on a Sunday so if anyone saw us we were told off.

I supported Cardiff City – they were a pretty good soccer team. We went down on special trains to Cardiff for the matches. We only ever had enough money for the train and the entrance to the match. There was no fun and games afterwards. We just came straight home again.

Although rugby was the traditional sport of South Wales, English immigrants into Wales brought the game of soccer with them, and it became increasingly popular.

Going to the cinema

I often went to the pictures in Tonypandy. There were two cinemas then, the Picturedrome and the Empire. Before the film started we went to the greengrocers and bought a halfpenny swede. Mother would peel it for us to eat in the cinema.

We sat in the "gods" upstairs on hard wooden planks with no backs to them. Then we used to hide in the toilets so we could see the film a second time around without paying! We were lucky then if we could afford to go each week but we didn't like missing an episode of the Saturday morning serial. The children's serial was so popular everyone called it the "penny rush". I liked the *Buck Rogers* serial – it would be on each week for months.

Flash Gordon was another children's film serial at this time.

There was a new *Tarzan* film almost every year throughout the 1930s and 1940s.

Film-going was so popular that queues used to form all down the street.

Radio days

We listened to the radio a lot at home. For a while we had piped radio from radio rentals. There were four wires running along the street and into each house down the outside wall. Indoors we had a box with a speaker and just one knob on it for the volume. Inside was a dry battery and an accumulator which had to be charged once a week.

There was one switch with three positions, middle was off, up was the Home Service and down the Light Programme. That was the choice then. We called it "home and away".

We liked listening to Big Band music; Henry Hall, Billy Cotton and *Saturday Night Music Hall*. We liked the comedians as well; Bennie Lyon, Gladys Morgan and a show called *Welsh Rarebit*.

The BBC was the only broadcasting station in the 1930s. The Home Service provided news and drama. The Light Programme covered popular music.

I really liked listening to Billy Cotton and his band on the radio.

The Coronation

The King's coronation in May 1937 was a great event for us. We were given a holiday from school since there were celebrations in all the streets. Just before the big day, the school gave out coronation mugs for the boys and coronation cups and saucers for the girls.

There were tables out in all the streets. Flowers and colourful flags decorated the streets. After we'd eaten the celebration meal there was dancing outside, to music from a wind-up gramophone. The party went on until it was dark. We only had a few gas lamps in the street so we went indoors quite early.

TIT-BITS CORONATION SOUVENIR

THEIR MAJESTIES KING GEORGE VI AND QUEEN ELIZABETH

After the coloured portrait by Peter North

SUPPLEMENT TO "TIT-BITS"

MAY 15, 1937

In 1937 George VI was crowned. The previous year his brother, Edward VIII abdicated in order to marry the divorcee, Wallis Simpson.

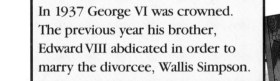

We had a big party just up the hill from us on Coronation Day.

CORONATION 1937

T.M. KING GEORGE VI AND QUEEN ELIZABETH

Build up to war

At home we listened to the wireless and heard the news of Hitler invading other countries. I remember hearing the British prime minister, Neville Chamberlain, saying, "I believe it is peace for our time", after he had met with Hitler in Munich. Lots of young men, including my older brother, went off to join up in the forces.

At school, we didn't take much notice until just before war was declared. The teachers told us to be prepared for air raid warnings and we had to practise air raid drill. The cellar of the school was turned into bomb shelters. We practised running in there with our gas masks.

I couldn't go into the forces myself, since by the time I reached the right age I was already working in the pit. The country needed coal to keep going during the war so I was needed there. I did join up as a volunteer firefighter later on but Tonypandy never was bombed. However, my sister, Gwladys, put out an incendiary bomb which hit the hospital where she was working in Cardiff.

Children throughout Britain were issued with gas masks. They were never actually needed.

Neville Chamberlain returning from Munich after meeting with Hitler.

Bomb shelters were quickly set up in the 1930s once war seemed definite.

Holidays

We never went away on holiday as a family. There wasn't enough money to stretch to that. The miners only got two weeks holiday a year, which was called "miners' fortnight". Even the pit-ponies had a break then. It was the only time all year that they saw life above ground.

In the August school holidays some of us boys used to go camping up on the mountain. We had to make our own tents. First we went to the Co-op and bought some of the big sacks that sugar came in. Then we cut them open and sewed them together to make simple tents. There'd be four or five of us boys in each one.

At Christmas there was always a funfair in Tonypandy. On New Year's Eve it would be absolutely packed. For half-an-hour after midnight, when the church bells and the factory hooter sounded, all the rides were free.

YOUR CHRISTMAS TABLE *Suggestions this Week*

WOMAN'S OWN AND WOMAN'S LIFE

2d

E-MADE SWEETS *are acceptable* GIFTS RECIPES

Mother made our Christmas pudding, of course. Christmas was also the only time in the year when we ate fresh fruit.

Pit ponies loading onto a train on the way to their "holiday".

Moving on

My sister, Gwladys, at the time she left home.

When I was twelve my sister Gwladys got married and moved out to Port Talbot. Her husband had a job in the steel works down there. Most girls round us went into service after they left school. They worked as maids for one of the colliery managers or went away to get a job in the house of a rich family. Gwladys and my other sister ended up nursing.

My older brother worked in the Gorki colliery for a bit. Then he signed up with the Royal Air Force just before the war.

After the First World War ended, the demand for coal was reduced. Many collieries were closed for some of the week.

My brother in his RAF uniform. He was one of the ground crew.

The depression

We were lucky that Father had work all through the 1930s. There was a lot of unemployment in the pits and nowhere much else to get a job. Most of the South Wales miners were on short-time working and families had very little to live on.

There were bad times when many people couldn't even afford breakfast. They'd go to the Salvation Army hall where there was sometimes free food. You could have bread, margarine and cocoa; or bread, jam and cocoa. You couldn't have margarine and jam at the same time.

Miners who were out of work couldn't get coal. They had to pick it off the mountain. This was illegal but the police usually turned a blind eye.

In 1936, unemployed shipyard workers marched 300 miles from Jarrow to London to draw attention to the problem of unemployment.

In the 1930s one in three men in the Rhondda were unemployed. Many families left to look for work elsewhere. Houses were just left empty.

Starting work

When I left school at fourteen I got a job through my uncle. He was the delivery man for the local bakery. I worked on the bread deliveries from seven in the morning until six in the evening, Monday to Thursday. Then on Friday and Saturday I worked until nine-thirty in the evening. For all this I earned seven shillings and sixpence a week. After a few months I started in the bake-house wheeling sacks of flour for fifteen shillings a week.

When I was fifteen my father had an accident in the colliery and broke both his legs. He was off work for some time and we didn't have enough to live on.

My wage from the bakery wasn't much so I went along, cap in hand, to the colliery manager to ask for a job. He said, "Does your father work here?". I said, "Yes, sir". He asked me my father's name and when I told him he said, "Start on Monday".

Miners were issued with a safety lamp before going underground.

FEATHERY FLAKE the quality Self Raising FLOUR

WHITE AND UNBLEACHED

HIGH GRADE FEATHERY FLAKE SELF-RAISING FLOUR MAKING VICTORIA FLOUR CO. BRISTOL

3-LB NET

For delightful puddings

Many deliveries were made by horse-drawn vehicles until the end of the 1930s.

OWENS & SONS Brynteg Bakery YSTRAD

We had to be careful about the rats getting our food underground. We used to hang our snap boxes on a hook to keep the food safe.

Payday at the colliery.

Father didn't want me to work down the pit so he was furious. If he'd been able to get out of bed he'd have stopped me going to see the manager.

I earned £1 2s. 6d. for a six day week. There were no guaranteed wages. If the pit was closed for any reason we got no money. We worked shifts of seven-and-a-half hours. You couldn't work the night shift until you were fifteen.

We had a twenty minute break for food which we took underground with us. I had bread and jam, or cheese sometimes. The jam kept the bread nice and moist.

A miner's life

I worked underground for eleven years until I developed dermatitis. My skin was really affected and the doctor said I couldn't work on the coal face any more. I got a job as a surface worker hauling the waste from the colliery around the slag heaps. When the Cambrian closed in 1966 I was put into a mobile team working on the rail tracks. I worked until 1980 when I was made redundant and couldn't find another job. I haven't worked since. I was considered too old at 55 to get another job.

My wife and I live in what was my mother-in-law's house up the hill from where I was born. I'm now deputy chairman of the local community committee. We've raised money to convert the old police station into a social centre. All that organising keeps me pretty busy.

My wife, Sally, and I on our wedding day in 1956.

The site of the Cambrian colliery now. There were fifty pits in the Rhondda Valley in the 1930s. Now there are none.

I was given a model miner's lamp as a retirement present.

In the News

These are some of the important events which happened during Glyn's childhood.

1930 In India, Mahatma Gandhi began a campaign of civil disobedience against the British colonial government.

1931 With the Western economy in trouble, Britain devalued the pound against the dollar. Sterling went from around $4.80 down to $3.40 to the pound.

1932 Franklin Roosevelt was elected President of The United States of America.

1933 Adolf Hitler became Chancellor of Germany. The Nazis began a violent campaign against any opposition.

1934 After an explosion in Wrexham pit, 262 miners lost their lives.

1935 Sir Malcolm Campbell set a world record of 301 mph in his car, Bluebird.

1936 Jesse Owens won four gold medals at the Berlin Olympic Games. Hitler refused to even shake his hand.

1937 The German air force bombed Guernica in Spain in support of the fascist government there.

1938 Adolf Hitler took control of Austria. Jews were not allowed to vote in a referendum on Austria's union with Germany.

1939 After Hitler's invasion of Poland, the British government declared war with Germany.

Things to do

Some of your relatives or neighbours will have memories of the 1930s. Their experiences may have been very different from those of Glyn Davies. Show them this book and ask them how their lives in the 1930s compared with his.

If you have a cassette recorder you could tape their memories. Before you visit people, make a list of the things you want to talk about – for example, toys and games, radio, films and sports. Most school leavers in the 1930s started work at fourteen. Find out what sort of jobs were available then. Ask about the different jobs done by men and women in the 1930s.

MAY 13, 1937

Daily Mirror

No. 10434

Registered at the G.P.O. as a Newspaper.   ONE PENNY

LONDON ED.

THE CROWNING OF GEORGE VI
KING AND EMPEROR

...he Dean of Westminster, places it reverently upon the King's ...ith loud and repeated shouts, cry, KING.''

Go to your local library. There may be a local studies section. Ask to see any photographs from the 1930s showing industry in your area. There may have been an established industry such as mining or manufacturing near where you live. Find out if it is still active.

Index

Series design: David Bennett
Design: Sally Boothroyd
Editor: Sarah Ridley

Acknowledgements: the author
and publisher would like to thank
Glyn and Sally Davies, Selwyn
Jones, Greg Reynolds, Bill Jones,
Dave Maddox, Ron Howells and
William John Thomas for their
help with this book.

Photographs: Cyril Batstone 8t,
10-11t, 15b, 24b, 25t; BFI Stills,
posters and designs 17br; Cynon
Valley Libraries 6br; Mary Evans
Picture Library 31b; Hulton
Picture Company 18b, 27b, 28b;
thanks to Byron Jones 25c; Kobal
front cover (bl), 17bl; thanks to
Llwynypia School 9c, 11t; thanks
to Mid-Glamorgan County Council
Education Authority 18c; National
Museum of Wales front cover (cl),
4bl, 6bl, 8b, 11b, 14b, 20b, 21b,
22b, 23t, 23bl, 24t, 25b; National
Museum of Wales/Spencer Powell
Collection 7tl; Robert Opie 6t, 7tr,
8c, 14t, 15t, 17t, 18t, 19c, 24c,
30br; Popperfoto 21t, 21c, 23br,
28tl, 29t, 29cl, 29b; Porthcawl
Museum 13b, 30cr; thanks to
Richard Shepherd 16; Neil
Thomson frontispiece, 5b, 9t, 12t,
26b; Topham Picture Source 27t,
27c, 28cr, 29cr; Treorchy Library,
Rhondda Borough Council 12c,
12b.

A CIP catalogue record for this
book is available from the British
Library.

Printed in the United Kingdom.